Understanding God Through:

Repentance,
Confession and Baptism,
Salvation

Velyn Cooper

Order this book online at www.trafford.com
or email orders@trafford.com

Most Trafford titles are also available at major online book retailers.

Printed in the United States of America.

ISBN: 978-1-4669-1494-0 (sc)
ISBN: 978-1-4669-1488-9 (e)

Trafford rev. 03/09/2012

 www.trafford.com

North America & international
toll-free: 1 888 232 4444 (USA & Canada)
phone: 250 383 6864 ♦ fax: 812 355 4082

Contents

Introduction

I am amazed at the amount of people who talk about God as if they are the best of friends, when they never spend any time reading his word or talking to him in prayer. It's like one person telling another person that they love them with all of their heart, yet they can never find quality time to spend with the person they claim to love so much. They operate strictly on their feelings. If they feel good today, God is the best thing since sliced cheese but if they are having a bad day, then God must have moved away from them. What is their problem? Unfortunately, their feelings vacillate or go back and forth between feeling good and connected to God and feeling bad and being disconnected from God. This boils down to one fact and that fact is that they really don't have a true relationship with God.

A true relationship with God takes place when we spend time with Him in prayer and in studying His word. This is not a 'when I feel like doing it kind of thing,' but something that we must practice daily, until it becomes a normal part of our lives. Think about it this way. You eat food everyday in order to nourish your body and keep you functioning properly and if you happen to miss a meal, within a few hours, you feel like you are going to pass out if you don't get something to eat. Well, it's the same way with the word of God. If you do not study the word of God on a regular and consistent basis, you will be spiritually malnourished and as a result you will end up malfunctioning spiritually.

When you look at the commercials on TV that show people who are less fortunate than you are, who are unable to get food on a daily basis, you actually see the lack of nourishment in their bodies. Little children have stomachs that are so big but they are big, not because they are filled with food, but because they lack food and are filled with air. That's how some of us are spiritually. We don't study the word of God on a regular basis and so we lack spiritual food. As a result, we are full of nothing but air. God's word is not in us and so we lack the power that we need from him, to live our lives in victory over sin. This causes another problem. Instead of growing in wisdom and knowledge of God and being able to teach others and lead them into a right relationship with him, through his Son, Jesus Christ, we need to be taught ourselves.

Hebrews 5:12-14 (King James Version)

[12]For when for the time ye ought to be teachers, ye have need that one teach you again which be the first principles of the oracles of God; and are become such as have need of milk, and not of strong meat. [13]For every one that useth milk is unskillful in the word of righteousness: for he is a babe. [14]But strong meat belongeth to them that are of full age, even those who by reason of use have their senses exercised to discern both good and evil.

Hebrews 5:12-14 (The Message)

[12-14] By this time you ought to be teachers yourselves, yet here I find you need someone to sit down with you and go over the basics on God again, starting from square one—baby's milk, when you should have been on solid food long ago! Milk is for beginners, inexperienced in God's ways; solid food is for the mature, who have some practice in telling right from wrong.

The Importance of Faith

It is very important to remember that our relationship with God is based on faith and not on feelings. How do we get faith? Faith comes by hearing and hearing comes by the word of God. (Romans 10:17, KJV)

So, if you are not studying the word of God you cannot have faith. You may get lucky from time to time and things work out for you but to have the God kind of faith that overcomes any situation, we must study His Word daily.

Now we begin our journey as this book takes us from repentance, confession and baptism to renewing our minds through the word of God.

On this journey, you will see familiar landmarks, as some of the lessons are tied into other lessons, creating a great format for becoming so familiar with the subjects being presented, that by the time you get to the end of the book, you should be able to effectively share its content with others.

Understanding God through Repentance

All of us at some point in our lives have done things that we have regretted. In some cases, they are things against our own selves but in most cases, they are things against others. Usually, we recognize the wrong we have done but the hardest thing for us to do is to apologize and seek forgiveness, especially when it us needing to forgive ourselves.

The worst prison in the world is the prison of un-forgiveness. It locks you in the solitary confinement of your mind, bringing to memory every sin you have ever committed; replaying them over and over again, until you feel like you are the worst person in the world and there couldn't possibly be any hope of you ever being free from this mess.

Suddenly, you have an epiphany and realize that you are the one holding the key that can release you from your self-imposed prison of un-forgiveness and that key is to repent of whatever wrong you have done; forgive yourself; where possible, seek the forgiveness of anyone you may have offended and then ultimately seek forgiveness from God.

John the Baptist

John the Baptist was the son of a priest named Zacharias and his wife Elizabeth. He was conceived when they were both very old. In fact, Elizabeth was so embarrassed about being pregnant at her age, that she hid herself from public view for five months.

John the Baptist had a very important role to play and for this role, he was filled with the Holy Spirit while he was still in his mother's womb. His filling of the Holy Spirit was a private event that was not physically witnessed by anyone, whereas when the Holy Spirit came and stayed upon Jesus at His baptism, this event was witnessed by John the Baptist and was the indicator to let him know that this Jesus was indeed the Son of God (Luke 1: 5-21; John 1: 32-34.)

The Holy Spirit also came upon the apostles and stayed upon them on the day of Pentecost, publicly identifying them as the apostles of Jesus Christ and empowering them for the ministry that was ahead. (Acts 2: 1-4)

Message of Repentance

John the Baptist's message was the baptism of repentance for the forgiveness of sin.

Luke 3:3 (KJV)
And he (John) came into all the country about Jordan, preaching the baptism of repentance for the remission of sins;

Why would John come preaching a message of baptism and repentance?

John came preaching a message of baptism and repentance because everyone born on this earth was born with a sin nature which we inherited from our forefather Adam and at some point, whether knowingly or unknowingly, we have sinned. Since we have all sinned, we all need to repent.

Romans 3:23 (KJV)
For all have sinned, and come short of the glory of God;

What does it mean to repent?

According to Encarta online dictionary, to repent means to :

- Recognize the wrong in something you have done and be sorry about it.

- Feel regret about a sin or past action and change your ways or habits.

In a nutshell, true repentance means recognizing that you have done something wrong; showing that you are genuinely sorry about what you have done by changing your ways and habits and as much as you are able to, not doing that thing again.

I don't want you to think for a second that once you are genuinely sorry about a wrong that you have done and you have repented and received forgiveness, that it means you will never do that wrong thing again. Unfortunately, because we are imperfect human beings, there are times when we make the same mistakes over and over again even though we are genuinely sorry every time we make them. I personally look at this as growing pains. Why? How many times do toddlers fall when they are learning to walk, yet they continue to get up and try and try again until they are walking perfectly? Now keep in mind that we went through those stages as we grew up but even now as adults, sometimes we still trip and fall. We break a little easier and hurt a lot more, yet we get up and continue on, even if we have to limp along for a while before we get our good step back.

Repentance is something like that. Sometimes you keep tripping and falling but you have to get up and keep on going—even when it is hard, you want to give up and it hurts to go on.

Godly Sorrow

To have Godly sorrow means to have true regrets about living your life or doing things that are outside of God's will, as outlined in His word; confessing your sin or shortcomings to him, accepting his forgiveness and continuing in a right relationship with him, through His Son, Jesus Christ.

2 Corinthians 7:8-10 (Amplified Bible)

[8]For even though I did grieve you with my letter, I do not regret [it now], though I did regret it; for I see that that letter did pain you, though only for a little while;

[9]Yet I am glad now, not because you were pained, but because you were pained into repentance [and so turned back to God]; for you felt a grief such as God meant you to feel, so that in nothing you might suffer loss through us or harm for what we did.

[10]For Godly grief and the pain God is permitted to direct, produce a repentance that leads and contributes to salvation and deliverance from evil, and it never brings regret; but worldly grief (the hopeless sorrow that is characteristic of the pagan world) is deadly [breeding and ending in death].

Based on the scripture above, we learn that Godly sorrow leads to repentance which then leads to a right relationship with God.

What Effect Does Repentance have on Us?

Repentance causes us to change from doing things our way to doing things God's way, as outlined in His written word—the Bible.

What Is Involved In Repentance?

Repentance involves a change of mind, a change of heart and a change of will.

A Change Of Mind

According to Encarta online dictionary, the mind is the center of consciousness that generates thoughts, feelings, ideas and perception, and stores knowledge and memories.

Sometimes, for no reason other than we have the ability to do so, we allow our thoughts to be negatively rather than positively focused. In other words, we pay more attention to the negative things people say and do and we always see the negative rather than the positive in situations and in people. The sad part is that this negative focus literally consumes us and causes us to miss out on some of the greater moments in life.

To keep our thoughts positively focused, the apostle Paul encourages us to think about positive things.

Philippians 4:8 (KJV)
Finally, brethren, whatsoever things are true, whatsoever things are honest, whatsoever things are just, whatsoever things are pure, whatsoever things are lovely, whatsoever things are of good report; if there be any virtue, and if there be any praise, think on these things.

Once our thoughts are positively focused, our feelings, ideas and perception or outlook will fall in line and become positive also. Out of this well of positivity will develop a character able to obtain and maintain positive knowledge and experiences and in so doing, will create positive memories.

If we all took on the challenge to be renewed in our minds, there would be no need for police officers or jails; the family structure would be as God designed it to be regardless of race, color or creed and we would all live in harmony with each other. Not to worry though, we may not experience this on earth at this time but all who have chosen to become a part of the family of God through Jesus Christ, his Son, will definitely experience this when Christ returns and sets up His kingdom on earth, where we will reign with Him as kings and priests.

Revelation 5:10 (KJV)

And hast made us unto our God kings and priests: and we shall reign on the earth.

A change of mind can only take place when we realize that we are not in a right relationship with God and we make a choice to come into a right relationship with him through his Son, Jesus Christ.

A Change of Heart

The heart is the source and center of emotional life, where the deepest and sincerest feelings are located and a person is most vulnerable to pain. (Encarta Online Dictionary)

Does this sound like the physical heart that pumps blood throughout our bodies? Does it remind you of a definition of another word we just studied? Think about it. Here is the definition of a word we just looked at that sounds a lot like the definition of the word, heart.

According to Encarta online dictionary, the mind is the center of consciousness that generates thoughts, feelings, ideas and perception, and stores knowledge and memories.

From the definitions given, does it sound like the mind and the heart are one and the same? In our way of thinking, our mind is where we formulate our thought processes and visualize past, present and future events and our heart is where we experience joy, suffering and pain. It appears that our physical heart literally aches when we lose a loved one to the cold hands of death and it appears to literally rejoice when something great happens in our lives. At least as far as we understand our physical heart to function.

What we need to realize is that our physical heart is a muscle that performs a physical function to keep us alive. It does not experience emotions as emotional experiences take place in the mind. Just like an engine is the heart of any machine, so the mind is the heart of a person. Hence the interchangeable use of the words mind and heart.

A change of heart (mind) takes place when we accept the fact that we are not in a right relationship with God and we do what is necessary to come into a right relationship with Him, through his son, Jesus Christ. We have to work at changing the focus of our minds from the things that we want to do, to doing the things that God requires of us, as outlined in His word.

Background Information
Passover

Passover is a Jewish Festival marking the exodus of the Hebrews (Israelites) from captivity in Egypt. (Encarta online dictionary)

The Israelites were in captivity (slavery) for four hundred (400) years. On the night of their deliverance from slavery, they were required to actively participate in their salvation, as it were, from Egypt. In the same way, we are required to actively participate in our deliverance from a life of slavery to sin, to salvation in Jesus Christ.

Exodus 12 (Amplified Bible)
[1]THE LORD said to Moses and Aaron in the land of Egypt,

[2]This month shall be to you the beginning of months, the first month of the year to you.

[3]Tell all the congregation of Israel, on the tenth day of this month they shall take every man a lamb or kid, according to [the size of] the family of which he is the father, a lamb or kid for each house.

[4]And if the household is too small to consume the lamb, let him and his next door neighbor take it according to the number of persons, every man according to what each can eat shall make your count for the lamb.

[5]Your lamb or kid shall be without blemish, a male of the first year; you shall take it from the sheep or the goats.

[6]And you shall keep it until the fourteenth day of the same month; and the whole assembly of the congregation of Israel shall [each] kill [his] lamb in the evening.

[7]They shall take of the blood and put it on the two side posts and on the lintel [above the door space] of the houses in which they shall eat [the Passover lamb].

[8]They shall eat the flesh that night roasted; with unleavened bread and bitter herbs they shall eat it.

[9]Eat not of it raw nor boiled at all with water, but roasted—its head, its legs, and its inner parts.

[10]You shall let nothing of the meat remain until the morning; and the bones and unedible (inedible) bits which remain of it until morning you shall burn with fire.

¹¹And you shall eat it thus: [as fully prepared for a journey] your loins girded, your shoes on your feet, and your staff in your hand; and you shall eat it in haste. It is the Lord's Passover.

¹²For I will pass through the land of Egypt this night and will smite all the firstborn in the land of Egypt, both man and beast; and against all the Gods of Egypt I will execute judgment [proving their helplessness]. I am the Lord.

¹³The blood shall be for a token or sign to you upon [the doorposts of] the houses where you are, [that] when I see the blood, I will pass over you, and no plague shall be upon you to destroy you when I smite the land of Egypt.

¹⁴And this day shall be to you for a memorial. You shall keep it as a feast to the Lord throughout your generations; keep it as an ordinance forever.

The sacrificial lamb paved the way of salvation from Egypt for the Jews and all others who participated in this act with them, just as Jesus Christ, the sacrificial lamb of God, paved the way of salvation for all who choose to believe in him today.

One Betrays, One Denies, One Repents and One Dies

The Plot to Kill Jesus

Betrayal

According to Encarta online dictionary, betrayal means to deliver somebody or something to an enemy.

Imagine that someone finds out that another person wants to harm you and they are willing to pay money to anyone who will be able to tell them where you are or to actually bring you to the person or bring the person to you. You will be amazed at how many people will actually betray you and hand you over for just a few dollars. I say a few dollars because you cannot put a monetary value on a human life.

Well, this is what happened to Jesus. The sad part about this is that he was not betrayed by a stranger but by someone who was an important part of his ministry.

Matthew 26:1-5 (KJV)

[1] . . . . he (Jesus) said to his disciples, [2]Ye know that after two days is the feast of the passover, and the Son of man is betrayed to be crucified. [3]Then assembled together the chief priests, and the scribes, and the elders of the people, unto the palace of the high priest, who was called Caiaphas, [4]And consulted that they might take Jesus by subtilty, and kill him. [5]But they said, Not on the feast day, lest there be an uproar among the people.

Matthew 26:1-5 (New Living Translation)

[1] . . . . he (Jesus) said to his disciples, [2] "As you know, Passover begins in two days, and the Son of Man will be handed over to be crucified." [3] At that same time the leading priests and elders were meeting at the residence of Caiaphas, the high priest, [4] plotting how to capture Jesus secretly and kill him. [5] "But not during the Passover celebration," they agreed, "or the people may riot."

The Jews still have high regard for the Jewish Holy Days. Not so with Christians as Holy Days for us have turned into Holidays.

Judas Agrees to Betray Jesus

Matthew 26:14-16 (NLT)

[14] Then Judas Iscariot, one of the twelve disciples, went to the leading priests [15] and asked, "How much will you pay me to betray Jesus to you?" And they gave him thirty pieces of silver. [16] From that time on, Judas began looking for an opportunity to betray Jesus.

Evil within will always find an avenue of release, if it is not harnessed by grace.

Jesus Predicts Peter's Denial and Repentance

Matthew 26:31-35 (NLT)

[31] On the way (to the Mount of Olives), Jesus told them, "Tonight all of you will desert me. For the Scriptures say, 'God will strike the Shepherd, and the sheep of the flock will be scattered.'

[32] But after I have been raised from the dead, I will go ahead of you to Galilee and meet you there."

[33] Peter declared, "Even if everyone else deserts you, I will never desert you."

³⁴ Jesus replied, "I tell you the truth, Peter—this very night, before the rooster crows, you will deny three times that you even know me."

³⁵ "No!" Peter insisted. "Even if I have to die with you, I will never deny you!" And all the other disciples vowed the same.

Emotional connections are always strong until they are put to the test.

Jesus Has foresight

Luke 22:31-34 (NLT)
³¹ "Simon, Simon, satan has asked to sift each of you like wheat. ³² But I have pleaded in prayer for you, Simon, that your faith should not fail. So when you have repented and turned to me again, strengthen your brothers."

Jesus knew that Peter was going to betray him; he also knew that Peter would repent and come back to Him. So you know what Jesus did? He told him that when he has repented and come back to Jesus, he must strengthen his brothers.

Of course, Peter vehemently or with great conviction declared that he would never deny Jesus, but in short order, that's exactly what he did.

Isn't it amazing that even though Jesus knew that Judas would betray Him and Peter would deny Him, He still treated them the same as He always did? Do you know why He was able to do this? He was able to do this because His love for them was unconditional. That's the kind of love we need to have for our fellow man. Unfortunately, that is easier said than done but is something we should all attempt to develop on a daily basis.

Peter Denies Jesus
(After his betrayal by Judas and his arrest)

Matthew 26:69-74 (NLT)

[69] Meanwhile, Peter was sitting outside in the courtyard. A servant girl came over and said to him, "You were one of those with Jesus the Galilean."

[70] But Peter denied it in front of everyone. "I don't know what you're talking about," he said.

[71] Later, out by the gate, another servant girl noticed him and said to those standing around, "This man was with Jesus of Nazareth."

[72] Again Peter denied it, this time with an oath. "I don't even know the man," he said.

[73] A little later some of the other bystanders came over to Peter and said, "You must be one of them; we can tell by your Galilean accent."

[74] Peter swore, "A curse on me if I'm lying—I don't know the man!" And immediately the rooster crowed.

Emotional connections usually fail when one's very survival depends on it.

Peter Has a Change of Heart

Matthew 26:75 (NLT)

Suddenly, Jesus' words flashed through Peter's mind: "Before the rooster crows, you will deny three times that you even know me." And he went away, weeping bitterly.

Godly Sorrow

According to Encarta online dictionary, to repent means to :

- recognize the wrong in something you have done and be sorry about it.

- feel regret about a sin or past action and change your ways or habits.

2 Corinthians 7:10 (paraphrased)

Godly sorrow leads to repentance

As soon as Peter became aware of the fact that he did indeed deny knowing Jesus Christ, godly sorrow kicked in and he wept bitterly. This was not sorrow with tears gently streaming down his cheeks in a nice sophisticated and pious manner; this was an all out break down as when people cry at the unexpected death of a loved one. He was truly sorry for what he had done and went on to be one of the great apostles of the ministry of Jesus Christ.

Judas Couldn't forgive Himself

Matthew 27:1-5 (NLT)

Judas Hangs Himself

[1] Very early in the morning the leading priests and the elders met again to lay plans for putting Jesus to death. [2] Then they bound him, led him away, and took him to Pilate, the Roman governor. [3] When Judas, who had betrayed him, realized that Jesus had been condemned to die, he was filled with remorse. So he took the thirty

pieces of silver back to the leading priests and the elders. [4] "I have sinned," he declared, "for I have betrayed an innocent man." "What do we care?" they retorted. "That's your problem." [5] Then Judas threw the silver coins down in the Temple and went out and hanged himself.

Unlike Peter, Judas did not experience godly sorrow—had he done so, he would not have gone out and hanged himself. He regretted what he did and the guilt he felt over what he had done was great; unfortunately, it wasn't the kind of guilt that leads to repentance but the kind of guilt that leads to escape from having to publically face up to your actions.

A Change of Will

Our will is our desire to do what we want to do, when we want to do it and how we want to do it. God gave us the freedom to exercise our will from the creation of man, when Adam was granted the freedom of choice in the garden of Eden. What we have to remember is that with the freedom to exercise our will comes consequences which will be either good or bad, based on the choices that we make.

Most of us don't like to accept responsibility for our actions because it always makes us feel so much better when we can blame someone else. Believe it or not, the best and quickest way to be free from past or present mistakes is to accept your responsibility for the role you played in your mistakes, forgive yourself and like the apostle Paul, move forward. Just remember that whatever you do, don't look back.

Philippians 3:13-14 (New International Version)
[13]Brothers, I do not consider myself yet to have taken hold of it. But one thing I do: Forgetting what is behind and straining toward what

is ahead, [14]I press on toward the goal to win the prize for which God has called me heavenward in Christ Jesus.

Changes of will take place when we make the decision to accept the teachings of God as outlined in His word and live our lives in accordance to His will and not according to our desires.

Why it is important for us to Repent

It is important for us to repent because there was a time when God overlooked our ignorance concerning him, but not anymore. Why? Knowledge of him is everywhere for anyone to access. If you cannot read, you can listen to the Bible via your computer, CD, MP3 player, iPod and so many more of the latest technological devices available. More importantly, He now commands us to repent because he has a day set aside when he will judge the world.

Acts 17:30-31 (Amplified Bible)

[30] . . . . He (God) charges all people everywhere to repent (to change their minds for the better and heartily to amend their ways, with abhorrence of their past sins), [31]Because He has fixed a day when He will judge the world righteously (justly) by a Man Whom He has destined and appointed for that task, and He has made this credible and given conviction and assurance and evidence to everyone by raising Him from the dead.

Who did God raise from the dead?

None other than Jesus Christ, therefore, God will judge the world through him. (Please note that Jesus Christ was the only person raised from the dead in his new and glorified body)

Why Jesus Came to Earth

Jesus came to earth to call the sinners to repentance

Matthew 9:13b (KJV)

for I am not come to call the righteous, but sinners to repentance.

Who are the sinners?

We are, which includes everyone who was ever born on this earth

Romans 3:23 (KJV)

For all have sinned and come short of the glory of God.

The Steps To Salvation

Repentance, Confession and Baptism
Go Hand In Hand

After hearing Peter's sermon on the day of Pentecost, when the Holy Ghost came upon them permanently, the people wanted to know what they needed to do in order to be saved. Peter's answer to them was:

Acts 2:38, 41 (KJV)
[38] . . . . repent and be baptized every one of you in the name of Jesus Christ for, the remission of sins . . .

[41]Then they that gladly received his word were baptized: and the same day there were added unto them about three thousand souls.

Remember that true repentance means recognizing that you have lived your life outside of God's will as outlined in his word; repenting of this, confessing this and being baptized in the name of Jesus Christ for the forgiveness of your sins.

Mark 16:15-16 (KJV) (Jesus is speaking to his disciples)
15) . . . Go ye into all the world and preach the gospel to every creature 16) He that believeth *and* is baptized shall be saved . . . .

Whenever persons in the Bible received the message of the gospel, it was presented to them in one sitting, after which, if they so chose, they were immediately baptized and were saved. Today, things are so different. Now, to get saved you have to go through so many man-made doctrines that take weeks and months to complete before you are able to be baptized. When did this all change? I guess this means that when you get baptized in this way, you are getting baptized into a doctrine of a particular denomination and not into Christ.

Do your own personal study of baptism as it is outlined in the word of God and baptism as it takes place in the denominational setting. I think you will find the results quite interesting.

Jesus' words were 'he that believeth and is baptized shall be saved.' This means that walking up to the altar and saying a prayer is not all there is to it. In fact, that is unscriptural and needs to be corrected immediately, if we want to follow the steps of salvation as outlined in the word of God.

Lets follow the steps to salvation in the conversion of the Ethiopian Eunuch (Acts 8: 35—38)

a) The Eunuch heard the word of God about Jesus

(Acts 8:35-38, KJV) Then Philip . . . . preached unto him Jesus

b) repentance of the Ethiopian eunuch—he believed the word of God about Jesus and desired salvation through baptism

Acts 8:36-37 (KJV)
36) And as they went on their way, they came unto a certain water: and the eunuch said, see, here is water, what doth hinder me to be baptized? 37a) And Philip said, If thou believeth with all thine heart, thou mayest.

c) Confession of the Ethiopian eunuch—he openly confessed his belief in Jesus Christ to Philip.

37b) And he answered and said, I believe that Jesus Christ is the Son of God.

d) The importance of openly confessing Jesus

Romans 10:9-10 (NLT)
[9] If you confess with your mouth that Jesus is Lord and believe in your heart *(mind)* that God raised him from the dead, you will be saved. [10] For it is by believing in your heart *(mind)* that you are made right with God, and it is by confessing with your mouth that you are saved. (Italics mine)

Confessing Jesus to others (telling others about Jesus)

Matthew 10:32-32 (KJV)
32) Whosoever shall confess me before men, him will I confess before my Father which is in heaven

33) But whosoever shall deny me before men, him will I also deny before my Father which is in heaven. (See also Luke 12: 8-9)

e) Baptism of the Ethiopian Eunuch

Acts 8:38 (KJV)
[38] And he commanded the chariot to stand still: and they went down both into the water, both Philip and the eunuch; and he baptized him.

The Significance of Baptism

Romans 6:3-4 (KJV)

3) Know ye not, that as many of us as were baptized into Jesus Christ were baptized into His death? 4) Therefore we are buried with Him by baptism into death: that like as Christ was raised up from the dead by the glory of the Father, even so we also should walk in newness of life.

Baptism signifies the death and burial of who we are outside of a relationship with Jesus Christ and our resurrection into our new life in Him.

Understanding God
through Salvation

What does it mean To Be Saved?

To be saved, in the biblical sense, means that you have been delivered, rescued or freed from sin by placing your belief/faith in Jesus Christ.

What Must I Do To Be Saved?

There is only one way to receive salvation and that is to repent and be baptized in the name of Jesus Christ for the forgiveness of sins, as we discussed in the previous chapter.

Paul, Silas and the Jailer

Paul and Silas were committed to their relationship with God. Wherever they travelled, they maintained their prayer life and their ministry of winning souls for the kingdom. They were always on call and nothing ever took precedence above their ministry of the gospel of Jesus Christ and the kingdom of God.

Let's see how a trip to the place of prayer landed them in a prison cell, resulting in the salvation of a man and his entire household.

Acts 16:16-34 (The Message Bible)
[16-18]One day, on our way to the place of prayer, a slave girl ran into us. She was a psychic and, with her fortunetelling, made a lot of money for the people who owned her. She started following Paul

around, calling everyone's attention to us by yelling out, "These men are working for the Most High God. They're laying out the road of salvation for you!" She did this for a number of days until Paul, finally fed up with her, turned and commanded the spirit that possessed her, "Out! In the name of Jesus Christ, get out of her!" And it was gone, just like that.

[19-22]When her owners saw that their lucrative little business was suddenly bankrupt they, went after Paul and Silas, roughed them up and dragged them into the market square. Then the police arrested them and pulled them into a court with the accusation, "These men are disturbing the peace—dangerous Jewish agitators subverting our Roman law and order." By this time the crowd had turned into a restless mob out for blood.

[22-24]The judges went along with the mob, had Paul and Silas's clothes ripped off and ordered a public beating. After beating them black-and-blue, they threw them into jail, telling the jail keeper to put them under heavy guard so there would be no chance of escape. He did just that—threw them into the maximum security cell in the jail and clamped leg irons on them.

[25-26]Along about midnight, Paul and Silas were at prayer and singing a robust hymn to God. The other prisoners couldn't believe their ears. Then, without warning, a huge earthquake! The jailhouse tottered, every door flew open, all the prisoners were loose.

Paul and Silas were so focused on their relationship with God that being in prison did not interfere with their ministry unto God. Their prayer meeting may have been interrupted but it wasn't cancelled; the venue may have changed but the event still carried on; the prison affected their physical location but their spiritual location was not moved. While in chains they prayed and they sang. Guess what happened? The power of God moved and physically loosed all of the prisoners. Were any of these other prisoners spiritually saved?

I don't know but they all benefited from the power of God and were physically freed from their chains.

27-28Startled from sleep, the jailer saw all the doors swinging loose on their hinges. Assuming that all the prisoners had escaped, he pulled out his sword and was about to do himself in, figuring he was as good as dead anyway, when Paul stopped him: "Don't do that! We're all still here! Nobody's run away!"

Without confirming the situation, the jailer went to the extreme and decided that he would take himself out before his bosses did. To his amazement, even though the opportunity was available, not one prisoner had left.

29-31The jailer got a torch and ran inside. Badly shaken, he collapsed in front of Paul and Silas. He led them out of the jail and asked, "Sirs, what do I have to do to be saved, to really live?" They said, "Put your entire trust in the Master Jesus. Then you'll live as you were meant to live—and everyone in your house included!"

The first question this previously unbelieving jailer asked Paul and Silas was what he needed to do in order to be saved. Their testimony, presented through prayer and hymn, set off a chain of events that caused this jailer to seek the salvation of God.

32-34They went on to spell out in detail the story of the Master—the entire family got in on this part. They never did get to bed that night. The jailer made them feel at home, dressed their wounds, and then—he couldn't wait till morning!—was baptized, he and everyone in his family. There in his home, he had food set out for a festive meal. It was a night to remember: He and his entire family had put their trust in God; everyone in the house was in on the celebration.

Even though they had been badly beaten, Paul and Silas ministered to the jailer and his family that very night and they were all baptized.

Ministry may be interrupted but the interruption should not cause you to stop ministering; in fact, it should cause you to press on no matter what.

What Must I Do To Be Saved?

The answer is the same no matter how often the question may be asked.

Acts 2:38 (KJV) (Peter is speaking)
. . . Repent and be baptized . . . in the name of Jesus Christ for the forgiveness of your sins . . . .

Mark 16:15-16 (KJV) (Jesus is speaking to his disciples)
15) . . . Go ye into all the world and preach the gospel to every creature.

16) He that *believeth and is baptized* shall be saved . . . .

Why Do We Need Salvation?

We need salvation because of sin.

Romans 3:23 (KJV)
For all have sinned and come short of the glory of God.

Through Whom Do We Receive Salvation?

We receive salvation through Jesus Christ.

John 3:17 (KJV)
For God sent not His Son into the world to condemn the world, but that the world through Him might be saved.

The cost of salvation for Jesus Christ—He died for us

Salvation is the gift of God that He offered to us freely but this gift cost Him the death of His Son, Jesus Christ.

Ephesians 2:8 (KJV)
For by grace are ye saved through faith; and that not of yourselves: it is the gift of God:

Ephesians 2:8 (Amplified Bible)
For it is by free grace (God's unmerited favor) that you are saved (delivered from judgment and made partakers of Christ's salvation) through [your] faith. And this [salvation] is not of yourselves [of your own doing, it came not through your own striving], but it is the gift of God;

The Cost of salvation to Us: We must die to self.

The wages or payment for sin is death and Jesus Christ died on the cross as the payment for all of our sins, so that we might receive the gift of eternal life.

Romans 6:23 (KJV)
For the wages of sin is death; but the gift of God is eternal life through Jesus Christ our Lord.

Romans 6:23 (Amplified Bible) For the wages which sin pays is death, but the [bountiful] free gift of God is eternal life through (in union with) Jesus Christ our Lord.

Once we accept Jesus Christ as our personal Lord and Savior, we too must die—we must die to self, to what we want to do—and live according to the Word of God by doing what His word says we should do.

The amazing thing is that even though Christ died thousands of years ago, His death covered everyone who was living at the time; those who were born after he died including you and me who are alive now and those who are still to be born. Now that's what you call power but more importantly, that's what you call unconditional love.

You Are Now a New Creation in Christ

Once you have believed, repented of your sins and been baptized, you are born again spiritually and are now a new creation in Christ.

2 Corinthians 5:17 (KJV)
Therefore if any man be in Christ, he is a new creature: old things are passed away; behold all things are become new.

Understanding God
through His family

Who is a part of the Family of God?

Those who have accepted Jesus Christ as their personal Lord and Savior through confession, repentance and baptism are a part of the family of God.

Confession

In this context, confession refers to declaring faith or belief in something or somebody. (Encarta online dictionary)

Romans 10:9-10 (KJV)
9) That if thou shalt confess with thy mouth the Lord Jesus and shalt believe in thine heart that God hath raised Him from the dead, thou shalt be saved.

10) For with the heart man believeth unto righteousness; and with the mouth confession is made unto salvation.

Repentance and Baptism Go Hand in Hand

Acts 2:38 (KJV)
Then Peter said unto them, Repent and be baptized every one of you in the name of Jesus Christ for, the remission (forgiveness) of sins . . .

Mark 16:15-16 (KJV) (Jesus is Speaking to his Disciples)

15) . . . Go ye into all the world and preach the gospel to every creature

16) He that believeth and is baptized shall be saved . . . .

Notice that Jesus stressed the fact that one must believe and be baptized in order to be saved. It is a package deal and one without the other will not work.

Some people might ask what happens if there is no water around for one to be baptized. Well, you can get baptized in your bathtub, your tin tub or in anything that can hold water. Trust me, God will give you the wisdom to know what to do if you are not in a position to get to a body of water to be baptized.

Who are the children of God?

Romans 8:14 (KJV)

For as many as are led by the Spirit of God, they are the sons (children) of God.

To be led by the Spirit of God, you must study the word of God. Why? How would you be able to identify the Spirit of God if you don't know anything about God from His word?

To identify something, you must know what it is beforehand. If you don't study the word of God, how are you going to be able to identify any of the actions of God? How will you know when His Spirit is dealing with you?

1 John 3:10 (KJV)

In this the children of God are manifest and the children of the devil. Whosoever doeth not righteousness is not of God, neither he that loveth not his brother.

1 John 3:10 (Amplified Bible)

[10]By this it is made clear who take their nature from God and are His children and who take their nature from the devil and are his children: no one who does not practice righteousness [who does not conform to God's will in purpose, thought, and action] is of God; neither is anyone who does not love his brother (his fellow believer in Christ).

Righteousness and love are two important aspects in having a right relationship with God. This is how the children of God are recognized and this also how the children of the devil—those who are not of God—are identified.

Righteousness means living your life according to God's standard, as outlined in His word—the Bible. It means doing what is right according to God and not to man.

Love means that you have deep positive feelings for someone and you care about them so much, that you will not intentionally do anything to hurt them.

Let's paraphrase 1 John 3:10.

This is how the children of God and the children of the devil are recognized. Those who live their lives according to God's standard as outlined in His word and love their fellow Christians so much that they will never intentionally do anything to hurt them, are the children of God. Those who are not of God do the complete opposite of those who are the children of God—they do not live their lives according to God's standard, as outlined in His word.

How do we know we are the children of God?

1) The Holy Spirit bears witness

Romans 8:16 (KJV)

The Spirit itself beareth witness with our spirit, that we are the children of God.

Romans 8:16 (Contemporary English Version)

God's Spirit makes us sure that we are his children.

Once we have given our lives to God, through His Son, Jesus Christ, the Holy Spirit becomes a part of us and confirms to us that we are God's children.

There will be times when you won't feel like you are one of God's children. When this happens, just remember that our relationship with God, through His Son, Jesus Christ is not based on feelings but on faith.

2) We keep His commandments

1 John 3:23-24 (KJV)

23) And this is His (God's) commandment, That we should believe on the name of His Son Jesus Christ and love one another, as He gave us commandment.

24) And he that keepeth His commandments dwelleth in Him (God) and He (God) in him.

God has two major requirements of us. One is that we should believe on the name of His Son, Jesus Christ and the other is that we are to love one another.

To believe on the Lord Jesus Christ is to follow His teachings as outlined in the word of God. To love one another, we should love, not by our words, but by our actions.

When we live in obedience to the commandments of God by following His teachings as outlined in His word, He actually lives in us and we live in Him and His Holy Spirit confirms in our hearts that He is indeed living in us.

Many people say that they believe in God, but their lifestyles show that while they believe in the existence of God, they don't follow the teachings of God.

You cannot believe in that which you do not understand. If you claim to believe in God, study His word so that you can truly understand who He is and live according to His teachings.

The Great Commandment

Matthew 22:37,39 (KJV) (Jesus is speaking)
37) Thou shalt love the Lord thy God with all thy heart, and with all thy soul and with all thy mind.

39) . . . . Thou shalt love thy neighbour as thyself.

We should love God with everything we have and not withhold any part of our lives from Him. We should also love our neighbor just as we love ourselves. It is apparent that many of us do not love ourselves because we sometimes treat others so unfairly.

Now the thing is, if you love God with everything you have—your heart, mind and soul—which He gave to you—you will not have a problem loving your neighbor as you love yourself. Why? How can you love God whom you have never seen and not love your neighbor, who you can see? I just pray that you treat your neighbors well because there is no better way of promoting the gospel of God's Son, Jesus Christ, than by showing love for your neighbor. (Please know that neighbor in this sense does not only refer to the people in the neighborhood where you live but to anyone you meet during your daily travels.)

What are the benefits of being a child of God?

We are heirs of God and joint-heirs with Christ. Everything belongs to God. In the beginning He had one Son, Jesus Christ and He was the sole heir of all that belonged to God. We, who have repented of our sins, been baptized and follow the teachings of Jesus Christ, our Lord and Savior, as outlined in the Bible, have been adopted into the family of God and have become joint-heirs with Christ. As a result, we will now share in the inheritance of Jesus Christ.

Romans 8:17 (KJV)

And if children, then heirs; heirs of God and joint-heirs with Christ, if so be that we suffer with Him, that we may be also glorified together.

If you have not yet repented of and been baptized for the remission of your sins, won't you consider doing so right now?

Acts 2:38 (KJV)

Then Peter said unto them, Repent, and be baptized every one of you in the name of Jesus Christ for the remission of sins, and ye shall receive the gift of the Holy Ghost.

Confessing versus Denying Christ

In **Matthew 10:32**, Jesus said that whoever confesses Him before men, He will confess before His Father which is in heaven.

Luke 12:8 (KJV) (Jesus is speaking)

Also I say unto you, Whosoever shall confess me before men, him shall the Son of man also confess before the angels of God.

Giving your life to Jesus Christ through repentance and baptism is only a part of the process of entering into a relationship with Him. Once you have become a part of the family of God, you now have a responsibility or obligation to tell others about Him. Now, if you want Jesus Christ to represent you before God, His Father, you must represent Him to the people you know and the people you meet. By doing this, you will be helping in the growth of the family of God.

All who deny Christ will be denied by Christ.

Matthew 10:33 (KJV) (Jesus is speaking)

But whosoever shall deny Me before men, him will I also deny before My Father which is in heaven.

Luke 12:9 (KJV)

But he that denieth Me before men shall be denied before the angels of God.

Point to Ponder

Please know that being a part of the family of God does not mean that you are going to be perfect and that everything is going to run smoothly all the time. As with any family, there will be disagreements among those who are a part of the family of God. Nothing is wrong with having disagreements; we just have to learn how to handle our disagreements in a godly way.

If you would like to contact the author, please send your questions
or comments to:

Velyn Cooper
P. O. Box F42524
Freeport, Grand Bahama
Bahamas

Email: biblicaljourneys@gmail.com
Website: biblicaljourneys.weebly.com

Follow us on Facebook and twitter